Presented to

_____

In appreciation for your service to the Lord

From

_____

Date

_____

*The heart of the giver makes
the gift dear and precious.*
~Martin Luther

*We always thank God for all of you,
mentioning you in our prayers.*
1 Thessalonians 1:2

Ripples

Of

Love

A Collection of Quotes, Scripture,
Poems and Prayers In Appreciation
for Those Who Serve the Lord

Christian Teacher's Aid

Providing Products To Help You Encourage God's People

Compiled by: Cathy Varvaris
Contributions by: Nancy Stallard, W. Michael Kilgore and Cathy Varvaris

CTA
P.O. Box 1205
Fenton, MO 63026-1205

1-800-999-1874

Printed in Thailand

Contents

1. *Ripples of Love:*

2. *One Small Drop:*

3. *God's Living Water:*

What we are is God's gift to us. What we become is our gift to God. ~Eleanor Powell

And my God will meet all your needs according to his glorious riches in Christ Jesus. Philippians 4:19

1

Ripples of Love:

God's Love Spreads Through Us

Let us not become weary in doing good, for at the proper time we will reap a harvest if we do not give up. Therefore, as we have opportunity, let us do good to all people, especially to those who belong to the family of believers. Galatians 6:9-10

God is not unjust; he will not forget your work and the love you have shown him as you have helped his people and continue to help them. Hebrews 6:10

The only ones among you who will be really happy are those who have sought and found how to serve. ~Albert Schweitzer

Ripples of Love

When a stone into the water is thrown,
Its circle soon grows beyond its own,
For a ripple can never stand alone.

Every ripple creates another,
Just like when you touch your brother,
You move him to reach out to others.

And you'll never, ever really know
How far your ripples of love go
All because, to God, you did not say "No."

*Lord, when I am discouraged,
remind me that you continue to work
long after my work is done. May I
only say "Yes" to the things that you
call me to do and then enable me to
trust you for the results.*

We make a living by what we get, but we make a life by what we give. ~Winston Churchhill

...Freely you have received, freely give.
Matthew 10:8

The best and most beautiful things in the world must be felt with the heart. ~Helen Keller

Preach the gospel always; if necessary, use words.

~St. Francis of Assisi

Since we live by the Spirit, let us keep in step with the Spirit.   Galatians 5:25

Dear Lord, remind me that the things I do will speak louder than anything I say. Help me to see others through your eyes of love.

I am a little pencil in the hand of a writing God who is sending a love letter to the world. ~Mother Teresa

...serve one another in love.
Galatians 5:13

You must be careful how you walk, and where you go, for there are those following you who will set their feet where yours are set. ~Robert E. Lee

People are like a stained glass window... their true beauty is revealed only if there is a light within. ~Elisabeth Kubler-Ross

...I am the light of the world. Whoever follows me will never walk in darkness, but will have the light of life. John 8:12

Father, let your light shine through me so others will see Jesus. May the light I shine always lead others to the safety of your harbor.

God comforts us not to make us comfortable, but to make us comforters. ~John Henry Jowett

Praise be to the God ... the Father of compassion and the God of all comfort, who comforts us in all our troubles, so that we can comfort those in any trouble with the comfort we ourselves have received from God. 2 Corinthians 1:3-4

Father, give me your compassion for those I serve. Help me to see their needs and then to show them that their real need is you.

One cannot give what he does not possess. To give love you must possess love. ~Leo Buscaglia

We love because he first loved us.

1 John 4:19

You can't lead anyone else further than you have gone yourself. ~Gene Mauch

The love we give away is the only love we keep. ~Elbert Hubbard

A new command I give you: Love one another. As I have loved you, so you must love one another. By this all men will know that you are my disciples, if you love one another. John 13:34-35

2

One Small Drop:

God Touches One Heart at a Time

Whatever you do, work at it with all your heart, as working for the Lord, not for men, since you know that you will receive an inheritance from the Lord as a reward. It is the Lord Christ you are serving.

Colossians 3:23-24

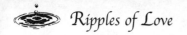

The highest reward for man's toil is not what he gets for it but what he becomes for it.

~John Ruskin

Whoever serves me must follow me; and where I am, my servant also will be. My Father will honor the one who serves me.   John 12:26

A Drop in the Bucket

Just today, I served another willingly for you.
But does it really matter when there's so much more to do?
Just a tiny drop into this bucket we call life,
One small act of kindness thrown amidst a world of strife.
But, by faith, I will believe and cast aside all doubt,
For I know that ripples from a single drop go out.
While on earth, I know that I will likely never see
Where or when or just how far those ripples go from me.
Daily, Lord, empower me these small, kind acts to do,
For in them, I can reflect the awesome love of you.
Fill me, Lord, renew my strength, my bucket overflow.
I want to be your useful tool wherever I may go.

It Began With One

It started with Jesus,
One drop of his blood,
It started as one drop
And welled to a flood.
His gift made your heart clean.
He made you his own.
Now you are his vessel,
To pass the gift on.
Go double the harvest,
Go spread his love out,
Go bless other people,
Go water the drought.

*Lord, thank you for touching my
heart. Make me sensitive to see those
in my life who need your touch. Use
me to reach them for you.*

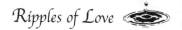

And whatever you do, whether in word or deed, do it all in the name of the Lord Jesus ... Colossians 3:17

The great leader is seen as the servant first.

~Robert K. Greenleaf

...serve the Lord your God with all your heart and with all your soul.

Deuteronomy 10:12

... my word that goes out from my mouth: It will not return to me empty, but will accomplish what I desire and achieve the purpose for which I sent it.

Isaiah 55:11

God doesn't call the equipped, he equips the called.

~Author Unknown

...the water I give him will become in him a spring of water welling up to eternal life.

John 4:14

The Living Stream

Your heartfelt, compassionate tear
Flows into the river of life,
And touches a weak, weary heart
Laden with both worry and strife.

The heart your life touches will stir,
Refreshed by the stream that flowed out.
It finds true compassion and love,
Where once there was worry and doubt.

Then that heart will broaden the stream,
And widen its loving embrace.
For waters will never run dry
When sent from the throne of God's grace.

Dear God, thank you for the living stream that flows in me straight from your throne. Lord, cause my life to bless others because they see you in me.

Daily Fill Your Buckets

It's not in one huge, single splash,
Our buckets are filled to the top.
God often will nourish instead
By filling our pails drop by drop.
May our God's love daily fill you.
May He your strength often renew.
So you can serve fully refreshed
And share that which He first gave you.

As the deer pants for streams of water,
so my soul pants for you, O God. My
soul thirsts for God, for the living God...
Psalm 42:1-2

3

God's Living Water:

Refreshed for Service

but whoever drinks the water I give him will
never thirst. Indeed, the water I give him will
become in him a spring of water welling up to
eternal life.   John 4:14

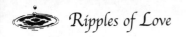

Ocean

Our world is an ocean
Tormented with sin.
We're tossed 'round by evils
Without and within.
But God made some ripples
And parted the sea
When He calmed those waters
And saved you and me.

*May the God of hope fill you with all
joy and peace as you trust in him, so
that you may overflow with hope by the
power of the Holy Spirit.*   Romans 15:13

He who is filled with love is filled with God Himself.

~St. Augustine

Whoever believes in me, as the Scripture has said, streams of living water will flow from within him.

John 7:38

Heavenly Father, remind me daily of the importance of coming to you to be refreshed by your living water.

My path cut through a desert place.
Wind-burned and parched, I fell.
My Jesus gently scooped me up,
His eyes with tears up-welled.
He spoke life to my barrenness—
Oases, fountains, springs!
His Word refreshes, overflows,
'Til deserts round me sing.

*Jesus stood up and said in a loud voice,
"If a man is thirsty, let him come to me
and drink. Whoever believes in me . . .
streams of living water will flow from
within him."*   John 7:37-38

*The Lord will guide you always; he will
satisfy your needs in a sun-scorched
land and will strengthen your frame.
You will be like a well-watered garden,
like a spring whose waters never fail.*

Isaiah 58:11

**Father, forgive me for always com-
ing to you as a last resort. Thank
you for your faithfulness to always
fill me, no matter what size cup I
bring. Help me to remember that you
desire to shower me with much
more than I can even imagine!**

As sure as ever God puts his children in the furnace, he will be in the furnace with them.
~Charles Spurgeon

When you pass through the waters, I will be with you; and when you pass through the rivers, they will not sweep over you. When you walk through the fire, you will not be burned; the flames will not set you ablaze.
Isaiah 43:2

Faith sees the invisible, believes the unbelievable, and receives the impossible.
~Corrie ten Boom

You cannot kindle a fire in any other heart until it is burning in your own.

~Anonymous

Father, fan the flames of my faith so that you will be seen in my life by those with whom I come in contact. Burn brightly in me, not only so that I will be warmed by your presence, but so others may be comforted by the glow.

Teach me, then, Lord, to bring to you, all that I may be, To all I do, my God and king, A consciousness of thee.

~George Herbert

...To him who is thirsty I will give to drink without cost from the spring of the water of life. Revelation 21:6

To keep the lamp burning, we have to keep putting oil in it.

~Mother Teresa

*Trust in the Lord with all your heart
and lean not on your own understanding; in all your ways acknowledge him,
and he will make your paths straight.*

Proverbs 3:5-6

**Dear Jesus, I find that just as my
appetite decreases when I go for long
periods without food, so my hunger
for your word decreases if I do not
feed my soul daily. Give me a hunger
for your word, Lord, that is only
satisfied by daily spending time with
you in your word. Thank you for
your faithfulness to always be there,
waiting for me to come.**

We are never defeated unless we give up on God.

~Ronald Reagan

Surely God is my salvation;
I will trust and not be afraid.
The Lord, the Lord, is my
strength and my song;
he has become my salvation.
With joy you will draw water
from the wells of salvation.

Isaiah 12:2-3

My flesh and my heart may fail, but God is the strength of my heart and my portion forever.
                                    Psalm 73:26

Relying on God has to begin all over again every day as if nothing had yet been done.
                                    ~C.S. Lewis

Lord, forgive me when I depend on my own strength. Teach me to rely on you. Be my strength for each day.

Thank You

While facing the world
As deep calls to deep;
When mountains ahead
Seem so high and steep;
I thank God you're there
To pull me along;
When I'm feeling weak,
He makes sure you're strong.
When my soul is bare
With nothing to glean,
I thank God for you,
On whom I can lean.
When my soul is dry
All withered and weak,
God gives you his words
To use when you speak.
When I'm feeling low,
When storms start to brew,
When I need a lift,
He leads me to you.
For you, I thank God,
Each day of my life.
You've doubled my joy
And lessened my strife.

You are God's fingerprint in the lives of others. He has touched others through you and they will never be the same.

~Cathy Varvaris

How can we thank God enough for you in return for all the joy we have in the presence of our God because of you?
1 Thessalonians 3:9

Dear Father, thank you for the people you have put in my path to encourage me. Through them I feel your love and presence. I know how much you love me each time I see them because they are a gift from you!

The Lord doesn't ask about
your ability, only your avail-
ability; and, if you prove
your dependability, the Lord
will increase your capability.
~Author Unknown

*...If anyone serves, he should do it with
the strength God provides, so that in all
things God may be praised through
Jesus Christ...* 1 Peter 4:11

God's Flow of Love

Just as it is impossible to stop the
Ripples of water once they start,

So it is impossible for Satan to stop our
Ripples of Love from reaching a heart.

Take comfort in that, and let Jesus'
Peace and Love flow.

Keep on dropping Love Pebbles
Every where that you go!

*...Well done, good and faithful servant!
You have been faithful with a few
things; I will put you in charge of many
things. Come and share your master's
happiness!*   Matthew 25:21

I thank my God every time I remember you. … being confident of this, that he who began a good work in you will carry it on to completion until the day of Christ Jesus.   Philippians 1:3,6

Lord, bless those who have blessed so many by their service for you. Meet every need they have. Guard and protect your servants from the enemy who would seek to destroy their spirit. Daily give them your strength and fill them with your Holy Spirit. Keep them morally and spiritually straight. Direct them so they will lead others to you. Bless the work of their hands so that your Son will be glorified in all they say and do. Amen.